SMOKE SIGNALS

100 years of tobacco advertising

PUBLISHED BY MIDDLESEX UNIVERSITY PRESS

SERIES INTRODUCTION

The twentieth century saw the advertising industry become a dominant driving force in Western culture. It was the engine of capitalism, directed political destinies and even influenced international conflict and military victories by means of propaganda. Advertising has become a defining element in our lives and culture, holding a mirror to our social history, values and aspirations.

'The historians and archaeologists will one day discover that the advertisements of our time are the richest and most faithful daily reflections that any society ever made of its entire range of activities' (McLuhan, 1964, p.247)

This book is one of a series which describes the history of twentieth-century printed advertising. Each publication focuses on a different product. Most illustrations for this series come from The Library of Historic Advertising (LHA), an extensive collection of twentieth-century printed advertisements owned by Middlesex University and housed in the archives at their Cat Hill campus, London.

CONTENTS

Introduction

The history of tobacco advertising during the course of the twentieth century is a story of conflict and struggle: companies battling with each other for new markets and then fighting against the claims of the links between tobacco and fatal illnesses and the consequent advertising restrictions. In the first half of the century, the industry developed its advertising to increase demand for its newly mass-produced product; in the second half, advertising was the primary tool used by tobacco companies to counter the negative health links and consequent decline in smoking. This book focuses on tobacco advertising as it appeared in popular magazines in both Britain and the United States of America. Advertisers developed different approaches to persuade the public to buy their product: style, design, humour, seduction, hope, flattery and snobbery; indeed, 'advertising imagery became the place where twentieth-century fantasies about the power of smoking to provide status, desirability or pleasure were defined' (Gilman, 2004, p.21).

There are two objectives for tobacco advertisers: to stimulate the initial demand for tobacco products and, thereafter, to increase brand loyalty. As mass production was introduced in the late Victorian period, manufacturers had to ensure that the demand met their huge outputs. They continued to persuade smokers into switching or remaining loyal to their brand by offering incentives such as cigarette cards or coupons, or by

Have you tried that
Extraordinary Cigarette

Herbert
Tareyton

"There's *something* about them you'll like"

TAREYTONS ARE A QUARTER AGAIN

ILLUSTRATION I

1926

"*That moment when you learn . . .*"

Men love women, and women love men, for the likes and dislikes they have *in common*. It can be a lifelong golden memory, that moment when you learn you both like the same play, hum the same tune when no one is listening, or smoke the same brand of cigarette. Not only (you chirp) because of the clean, firm feel of Craven 'A''s *natural* cork tip, so kind to the lips, and the rare, unvarying flavour of the rich, fine tobacco, so kind to the throat! *She* (or *he*) smokes them, too! As if anyone else, or any other cigarette, could matter, after that.

Those who smoke Craven 'A'
seldom care for other cigarettes

ILLUSTRATION 2

John Bull, 1950

ILLUSTRATION 3

1937

ILLUSTRATION 4

Vogue, 1981

MIDDLE TAR As defined by H.M. Government
DANGER: H.M. Government Health Departments' WARNING:
CIGARETTES CAN SERIOUSLY DAMAGE YOUR HEALTH

persuading the consumer to identify with a certain brand image. Campaigns were developed that gave individual brands identities reflecting personal aspirations and social class. Woodbine cigarettes in Britain were associated with solid working-class men, Craven 'A' cigarettes were more ladylike and du Maurier was positively upper class. In America, the brand of cigarette you smoked often marked you as a fan of a particular baseball team: New York Giants fans would probably smoke Chesterfield, a Yankee fan Camels and Lucky Strike would be preferred by Dodgers supporters (Blum, 1988, p.21).

The industry developed into a massive worldwide presence with millions of people dependent on tobacco for their livelihood – producers, transporters, advertisers, publishers, retail outlets, sponsored sports and arts, and of course governments, who benefit from the income from the most heavily taxed consumer product in the world.

Opposition and obstacles to widespread tobacco use have taken many forms over the century; temperance movements, social unacceptability for women to smoke, clean-air campaigns and of course, in the second half of the century, the evidence linking smoking with cancer and other deadly illnesses. Nevertheless, in the face of all this negativity, tobacco advertising has succeeded in giving the smoker the image of glamour, independence, maturity, emancipation, beauty, sociability, self-assurance and even health. But advertisers have had to work hard, and pay hard – more money has been spent on tobacco advertising in the twentieth century than the advertising of any other product. Tobacco consumption in the West has decreased since its peak in mid-century; however, the markets in the developing world have not yet been fully exploited and the expertise in persuasion developed over the last century will inevitably be used to full effect this century.

Chapter 1

1900–1920

Black Cats, Camels
and the 'Tommies'

This period saw a huge increase in spending on advertising by tobacco companies who particularly saw the benefits of advertising in magazines. John Player & Sons, for example, were spending £55,750 on advertising in 1911 and by the mid-1920s they were spending around £500,000 each year. Printing techniques and reproduction quality were improving and attractive, well-designed advertisements were being seen as adding appeal to a magazine.

At the turn of the nineteenth century, pipe smoking was being displaced slowly by cigarettes. Tobacco manufacturers had invested in cigarette-making machines towards the end of the century which had ended the reputation of the cigarette as an expensive, elite, hand-rolled product exclusively meant for the very wealthy. Because of mass production, manufacturers had to ensure that consumers purchased their goods in numbers similar to that at which technology allowed cigarettes to be manufactured. In order to achieve this, they invested in advertising on a grand scale. Magazines and newspapers such as *Strand*, *Answers* and the *Daily Mail* had huge circulations each of around one million towards the end of the nineteenth century. At one point, *Strand Magazine* had one hundred pages of advertisements per issue. Tobacco companies saw the opportunity to target readers and get their product noticed. Rather than matching their product with a particular target group, companies tried to appeal to a broad range of the

646.09

MILITARY UNIFORMS
OF THE
BRITISH EMPIRE
OVERSEAS

R. Roe

AN ALBUM OF
SEA FISHES

ISSUED BY

...YER & SONS

...IAL TOBACCO COMPANY
...D IRELAND), LIMITED

58 fibe 27

PRICE ONE PENNY

WILLS'S
CIGARETTE
PICTURE-CARD
ALBUM

The Navy

PRICE ONE PENNY

ILLUSTRATION 5a
1930s

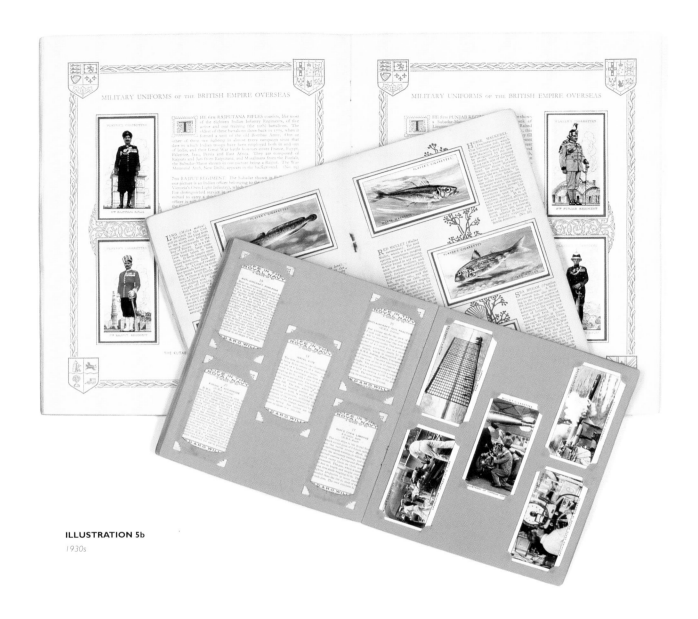

ILLUSTRATION 5b

1930s

population using familiar and traditional icons to promote their products. They employed themes such as patriotism, empire, monarchy and a sense of British heritage, especially in pipe tobacco. In 1901, there were thirteen brands of pipe tobacco in Britain with the word 'Old' in the title. Cigarette cards were starting to be issued as well at this time in order to encourage brand loyalty. The collectable images generally followed traditional, military and royal themes and proved very successful, enduring for several decades **ILLUSTRATIONS 5a, 5b.**

THE "CADET."

They do put us through it; since I left Marlboro' I have never had to work as I have done lately: why, settling days on the Stock Exchange are nothing to it. Not having touched mathematics for years, the exams. seem a bit "up to you" at first; but I have learnt one thing—all the wise ones smoke "Army Clubs." They're dinkie!

CAVANDER'S
"Army Club"
CIGARETTES

20 for 9d.   50 for 1/10½.   100 for 3/9.

Packets of 10 can be obtained in those convenient paper pockets for 4½d.

For a mellow non-bite Tobacco try
CAVANDER'S "ARMY" MIXTURE
7½d. per oz.   2/6 per ¼-lb. tin.

CAVANDERS, Glasgow.   The Firm of Three Centuries.

ILLUSTRATION 6

The Sphere, 1905

—*but you can't hide the* <u>taste</u> *!*

"That good old Fatima taste!"—hundreds of thousands of men throughout the entire country know it. And swear by it.

Most of those men had their troubles before they tried Fatima. They shopped around. They tried brand after brand—different kinds—different prices.

Yet, nothing quite touched the spot—until FATIMA. There—in Fatima—they found what they'd been

hoping and longing and searching for in a cigarette. Fatima is mild—*generously* mild, with a mellowness and "character" that blend smoothly in every delicious puff. *You can't hide that taste!*

Three men smoke Fatimas to every one *who calls for any other 15c cigarette. Three to one—think of it! Next time why don't you choose Fatimas and see if they don't exactly suit your taste, too?*

Liggett & Myers Tobacco Co.

The Cigarette with 3 times as many friends

FATIMA
THE TURKISH BLEND
Cigarette

20 *Distinctively Individual* 15¢
FATIMAS

ILLUSTRATION 7

Saturday Evening Post, USA, 1915

Nevertheless, there were some companies that aimed to appeal to class-conscious customers, pandering to snobbery and class differences to make their product appealing. An Army Club advertisement associates its product with a public school ('Marlboro' refers to the Marlborough College, a public school in Wiltshire) and the officers' mess **ILLUSTRATION 6**.

The popularity of Turkish and Egyptian cigarettes had grown enormously up to the beginning of World War One and advertisements for brands such as Fatima **ILLUSTRATION 7** and Mogul gave the opportunity for magazine advertising to produce imagery of the romantic orient **ILLUSTRATION 8**.

This period also saw the development of branding. Companies were beginning to give their products a 'personality', one that stood out in the shop and that customers could recognise. The brand images had the potential to appeal to a broad range of consumer. Black Cat became an iconic brand image and the first big budget advertising campaign for cigarettes in America in 1914 was for Camel cigarettes **ILLUSTRATION 9**. The camel has endured as a brand icon for nearly a century. It was originally chosen as a symbol of exoticism and as representing the region from which Turkish tobacco originated. This is despite the fact that there are neither camels nor pyramids in Turkey!

Existence de Luxe

with
ABDULLA SUPERB CIGARETTES
TURKISH · EGYPTIAN · VIRGINIA

ILLUSTRATION 8

Punch's Almanack for 1929, 1928

ILLUSTRATION 9

1915

CAMEL CIGARETTES

Are Here!

R. J. REYNOLDS TOBACCO CO., Winston-Salem, N. C.

To Cigarette Smokers of America

Camels have arrived! Here is a cigarette made of *blended* choice Turkish and choice Domestic tobaccos that produce a finer flavor, a better fragrance, than either kind of tobacco smoked straight!

Camel Cigarettes *will not* sting the tongue and *will not* parch the throat. They *do not* leave any unpleasant cigaretty after-taste.

Compare Camels for quality, for flavor, with any cigarette in the world! *And make your comparison today!*

Please note that Camel packages contain neither coupons nor premiums. Smokers do not look for them, because they realize that the cost of the tobaccos prohibits their use.

Men who do the Empire's Work. No. 1—Lord Kitchener.

IN concentrating on gigantic problems such as never before assailed a human
brain, it is at least conceivable that "The Man at the Helm" should sometimes
seek the soothing influence of "My Lady Nicotine"—perhaps Craven "A."

For there is no finer tobacco than Craven, and Craven "A" is its brother.

Craven "A" follows the original, secret Craven blend, to which it owes its rich,
mellow flavour, its smooth mildness in smoking, and its delightful fragrance.

The taste for Craven "A" does not need acquiring, it will suit you from the
very first puff, and be a revelation in flavour, sweetness, and fragrance.

Put Craven "A" in your pipe to-day, and you will immediately agree that
there is no tobacco to equal it at anywhere near the price of 6d. per ounce.

CRAVEN "A"
MIXTURE
"Sixpence an ounce"

Obtainable of all first-class tobacconists, and at 55, Piccadilly, W., and 7, Wardour St., Leicester Sq., W., in
1-oz. and 2-oz. packets at 6d. per oz., and in hermetically sealed tins (with damper), 4 oz., 2/-; 8 oz., 4/-.
CARRERAS, LTD. (Established 1788), ARCADIA WORKS, LONDON, E.C.
Craven "A" Cigarettes, Virginia (plain or cork tipped), in tin boxes, 25 for 1/-.
The ideal Cigarette for Ladies and Gentlemen.

ILLUSTRATION 10
The Graphic, 1915

Player's Navy Cut
Tobacco & Cigarettes
FOR THE TROOPS.
From all quarters we hear the same simple request:
"SEND US TOBACCO AND CIGARETTES."

TROOPS AT HOME   **(Duty Paid)**

It would be well if those wishing to send
Tobacco or Cigarettes to our soldiers would
remember those still in Great Britain. There
are thousands of Regulars and Territorials
awaiting orders, and in sending a present
now you are assured of reaching your man.

Supplies may be obtained from the usual
trade sources and we shall be glad to
furnish any information on application.

TROOPS AT THE FRONT   **(Duty Free)**

John Player & Sons, Nottingham, will
(through the Proprietors for Export, The
British-American Tobacco Co., Ltd.) be
pleased to arrange for supplies of these
world-renowned Brands to be forwarded
to the Front at Duty Free Rates.

JOHN PLAYER & SONS,
Castle Tobacco Factory,
Nottingham.

Branch of the Imperial Tobacco Co. (of Gt. Britain & Ireland) Ltd.

ILLUSTRATION 11
Punch, 1915

In America by 1915, the consumption of cigarettes increased to over sixteen billion from just over two billion in 1890, and by that time the American tobacco industry was employing around 200,000 people. In opposition there was a powerful temperance movement and the National Anti-Cigarette League, formed in 1901, was at the forefront of the anti-tobacco movement. In partnership with some business leaders such as Henry Ford, who regarded smoking as a deterrent to worker productivity, the League succeeded in achieving many legislative controls of the sale of tobacco and smoking.

Nevertheless, many were not enforced and were repealed by 1927 (Greaves, 1996, p.17). There was a similar movement in Britain. Organisations such as the British Anti-Tobacco League and the International Anti-Cigarette League which had 80,000 young members in 1908 who had pledged not to smoke, at least until the age of twenty-one. In Britain, these organisations had less success in influencing national legislation, not even able to push through terms which would have made it illegal to sell tobacco to young people under sixteen (Hilton, 2000, p.168).

ILLUSTRATION 12

The Sphere, 1917

"*Two Bars Rest*"

E. LUCCHESI

World War One provided tobacco manufacturers with an opportunity to broaden the appeal of cigarettes even further. Companies, such as Imperial Tobacco in Britain, gave cigarettes to the government to pass on to the armed forces, converting many young soldiers – known as 'Tommies' – to the habit. The British government regarded the smoking of cigarettes as a reliever of boredom and stress for those on the front line. Advertising for the home front linked smoking with patriotism and support for the troops **ILLUSTRATIONS 10, 11**. This period also saw a decline in the use of Turkish tobacco in America as a patriotic preference to use tobacco from the Eastern states increased.

Up to the 1920s, it was generally considered socially unacceptable for women to smoke and the cigarette was regarded as a 'badge of questionable character …between the lips of a woman' (Barnard, 1929, p.6). Indeed, there were some local and regional laws in America prohibiting smoking by women in public. In 1904, a policeman in New York arrested a woman for smoking a cigarette in a car, 'You can't do that on Fifth Avenue' (Ernster, 1985, p.335). Because of this social climate, tobacco advertisers did not suggest that their product should appeal to women and it was very unusual for a woman to be portrayed as smoking a cigarette in advertisements before 1927. This advertisement for De Reszke cigarettes is a notable exception **ILLUSTRATION 12**.

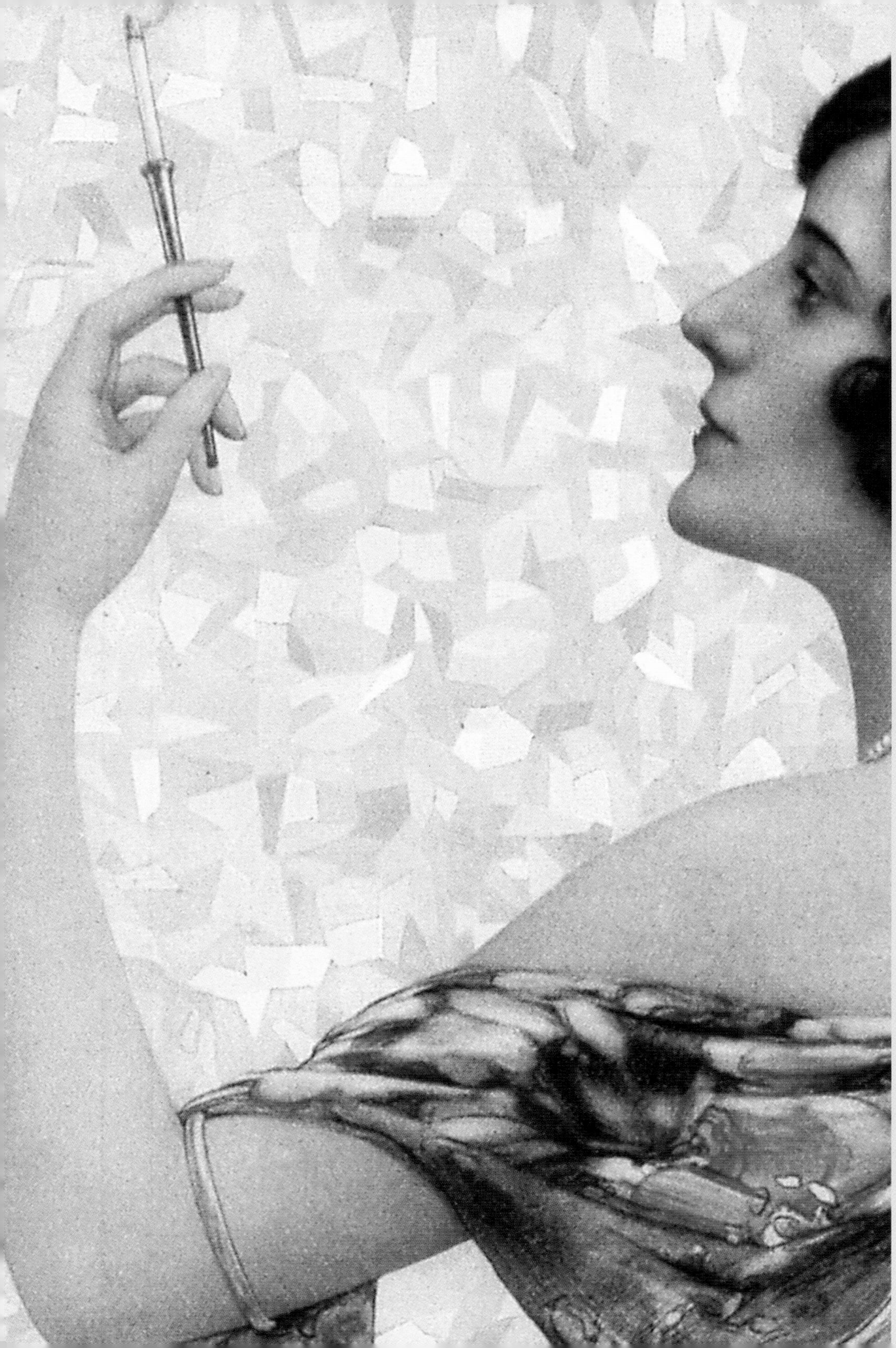

Chapter 2

1920s

Stylish, slender and
sophisticated

This was an economic boom period in both Britain and the USA. Profits were soaring and companies were increasing their investment in advertising. Higher standards of visual design could be seen in advertising with more advanced reproduction techniques and the influence of Art Nouveau and Modernist styles. The Three Nuns advertisement reveals the influence of Art Deco design from that period ILLUSTRATION 13. Even the text reflects the emphasis on new creativity and invention during the 1920s. Some designers realised that the impact of advertisements could be more direct and eye catching if they reduced the amount of text. This State Express 555 advertisement from 1923 illustrates this change ILLUSTRATION 14. Advertisers were engaging fine artists to create striking visual images such as this Player's advertisement from 1929 ILLUSTRATION 15.

During the 1920s, the rise in lung cancer among Americans was first noted. The death rate had increased from 0.6 per 100,000 people in 1914 to 1.7 in 1925. This was a low statistic compared to other killers such as influenza and tuberculosis, but because figures tended to be higher in urban areas and among men, links were suggested between lung cancer and certain occupations such as carpentry, mining or metal processing and even the rise in automobile traffic and its emissions. The conclusion of a study by Frederick Hoffman in 1929 in the *American Review of Tuberculosis* reflected the public and government views. It stated that, 'there is no definite

THERE *is a tobacco especially favoured among writers and artists and others whose work is of the creative kind. They smoke Three Nuns—smoke it prodigiously; and are willing to pay for it a penny or so an ounce more than for ordinary tobaccos, because they know what inspiration, what solace, what freedom from distraction that extra penny buys. In the rare cool fragrance imprisoned in the cunningly blended coils of Three Nuns lies the never-to-be-resisted lure of a faultless pipe tobacco.*

THREE NUNS
The Tobacco of Curious Cut
1'2
an ounce

Stephen Mitchell & Son, Glasgow. Branch of The Imperial Tobacco Co. (of Great Britain and Ireland), Ltd.

ILLUSTRATION 13
Punch, 1927

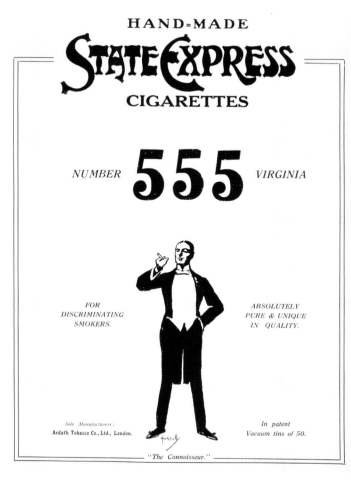

ILLUSTRATION 14
The Times of India Annual, 1923

evidence that smoking habits are a direct contributory cause toward malignant growths in the lungs' (Kluger, 1996, p.71).

Nevertheless, advertisers seemed conscious of health implications and emphasised 'mildness', 'protection' and that smoking their product would not irritate or cause coughs. The text of a Lucky Strike advertisement from 1930 illustrates this, 'Your throat protection — against

ILLUSTRATION 16

1930

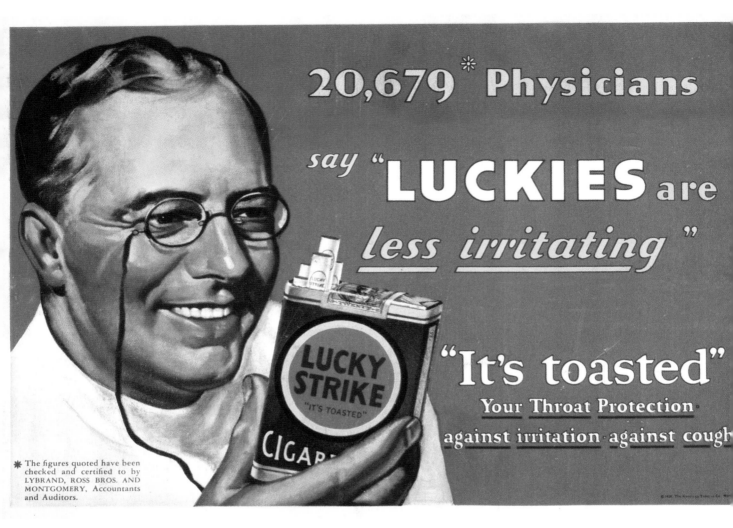

ILLUSTRATION 17

1930

irritation – against cough' ILLUSTRATION 16. Lucky Strike used doctors' endorsements in their advertising. The company offered American doctors five free cartons if they agreed that 'Luckies' were the least abrasive brand. The resulting slogan was, '20,679 physicians say Luckies are less irritating' ILLUSTRATION 17.

Lucky Strike also exploited the link between losing weight and smoking – a tobacco selling point that would endure throughout the century. Their famous campaign, 'Reach for a Lucky instead of a sweet' implied that women could control the intake of fattening foods by smoking. The dress fashion of the time certainly suited a slimmer figure,

ILLUSTRATION 18

Punch, 1928

"TRIM LITTLE CRAFT"

PLAYER'S
NAVY CUT
CIGARETTES
PLAIN, OR TIPPED WITH CORK OF PURE NATURAL GROWTH

REALLY NICE GIRLS SMOKE **PLAYER'S CORK-TIPPED**

Charming

Player's cork-tipped Please!

10 *for* 6ᴰ · 20 *for* 11½ᴰ · 50 *for* 2/5

PLAYERS NAVY CUT

IT'S THE TOBACCO THAT COUNTS

ILLUSTRATION 19
Punch, 1928

as shown in the British Player's Navy Cut advertisement with its unsubtle play on words, 'trim little craft' ILLUSTRATION 18. The confectionery industry inevitably protested and the slogan was changed to 'When tempted, reach for a Lucky instead' (see Illustration 16, Lucky Strike). Sales went up 215 per cent and the brand became America's best-selling cigarette in just two years (American College of Chest Physicians, 2004, p.1).

During the 1920s, tobacco manufacturers thought to exploit the growing independence and emancipation of women by working to change the traditional view that respectable women should not smoke. Women began to be shown in cigarette advertisements later in the decade. In the United States in 1923, 5 per cent of all cigarettes were consumed by women, which had increased to 12 per cent by 1929 (Ernster, 1985, p.336). The Player's advertisement with the phrase, 'Really nice girls smoke Player's cork-tipped' ILLUSTRATION 19, was a clear attempt to show that women need not compromise their reputation if they smoked. The Will's Gold Flake advertisement ILLUSTRATION 20 emphasises the attempt to represent women smokers as pure and 'good', with the inclusion of dolls and toys which gave the model a childlike innocence.

By the end of the decade advertisers had succeeded in establishing the association of smoking with style, sophistication and fashion for both men and women ILLUSTRATIONS 21, 22 – quite an achievement.

ILLUSTRATION 21

The Illustrated London News, 1928

ILLUSTRATION 22

Punch, 1928

Chapter 3

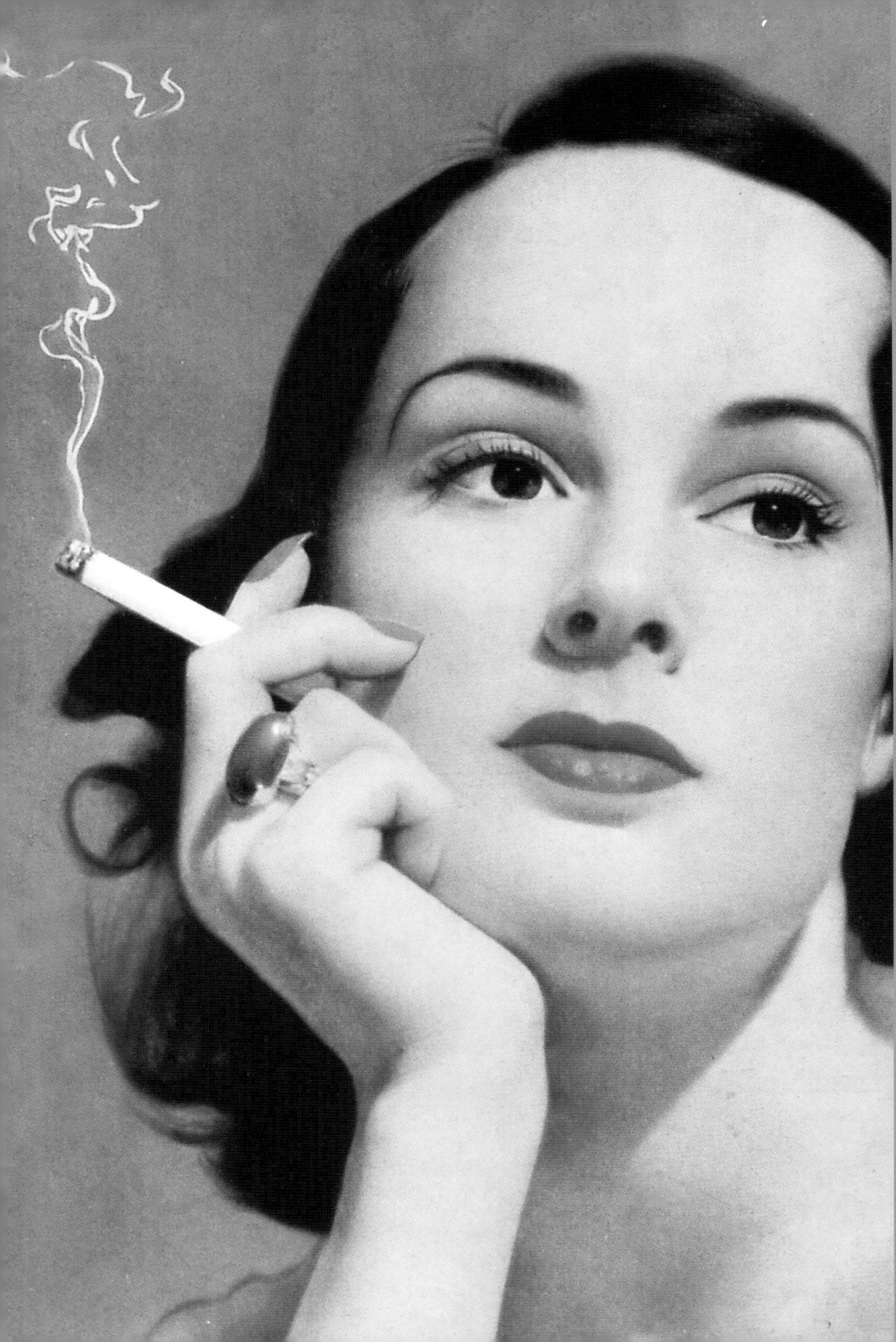

1930s

The carefree
smoker

The 1930s was a period of economic depression in both Britain and the United States, but there is little sign of this in tobacco advertising. Tobacco advertising in the 1930s, like motion pictures of the time, brought glamour, romance and fashion. The Craven 'A' and Wills's Gold Flake advertisements ILLUSTRATIONS 23, 24 epitomise the image of the carefree smoker – smoking as an escape from the problems of economic recession. Tobacco companies were also attempting to associate smoking with wealth and upward social mobility. A Camel advertisement from 1934 ILLUSTRATION 25 was part of a large American campaign to associate the brand with high society and to finally dispel the traditional view of smoking being socially unacceptable for women. The Chesterfield advertisement spells out how women smokers were associated with emancipation and independence ILLUSTRATION 26.

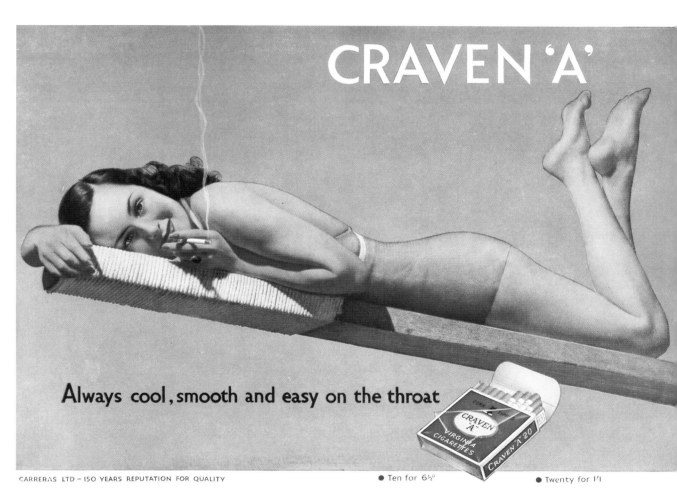

CRAVEN 'A'

Always cool, smooth and easy on the throat

CARRERAS LTD – 150 YEARS REPUTATION FOR QUALITY   ● Ten for 6½ᵈ   ● Twenty for 1/1

ILLUSTRATION 23

Britannia and Eve, 1939

ILLUSTRATION 24

Punch, 1930

MRS. J. GARDNER COOLIDGE, 2ND

Three things women enjoy especially in smoking Camels

"I enjoy their full, rich flavor," says Mrs. J. Gardner Coolidge, 2nd ••• "They never make my nerves jumpy," reports Mrs. Thomas M. Carnegie, Jr. ••• "They are smooth and mild," adds Mrs. James Russell Lowell ••• Again and again women make these same points about Camels.

"I find Camels delightfully mild," agrees Mrs. Potter d'Orsay Palmer ••• "Camels never make me nervous," Miss Alice Byrd says. "I like their taste better," states Miss Anne Gould ••• Why don't *you* see if your nerves and taste aren't exactly suited by Camel's costlier tobaccos?

CAMELS ARE MADE FROM
FINER, <u>MORE</u> EXPENSIVE <u>TOBACCOS</u>
THAN ANY OTHER POPULAR BRAND

MRS. JAMES RUSSELL LOWELL

Camel's costlier tobaccos appeal to

Miss Mary Byrd
Miss Alice Byrd
Mrs. Powell Cabot
Miss Anne Gould
Mrs. Potter d'Orsay Palmer

MRS. THOMAS M. CARNEGIE, JR.

ILLUSTRATION 25
1934

I really don't know if I should smoke . . .

. . . but my brothers and my sweetheart smoke, and it does give me a lot of pleasure.

Women began to smoke, so they tell me, just about the time they began to vote, but that's hardly a reason for women smoking. I guess I just like to smoke, that's all.

It so happens that I smoke CHESTERFIELD. They seem to be milder and they have a very pleasing taste.

the Cigarette that's Milder

the Cigarette that Tastes Better

ILLUSTRATION 26
1933

This year give **du MAURIER** in this special Christmas packing

ILLUSTRATION 27
1936

— before you go up

WILL'S **STAR** CIGARETTES
10 for 4ᵈ 15 for 6ᵈ 30 (in box) 1/-
PLAIN OR CORK TIPPED

ILLUSTRATION 28
John Bull, 1936

Improved reproduction techniques and the glamorisation of advertising resulted in some visually exciting images. The du Maurier advertisement from 1936 cleverly represents style and beauty with the use of just red, silver and black **ILLUSTRATION 27**. There was improved experimentation in advertising styles and techniques in the 1930s. A woodcut for Wills's Star cigarettes by Alex Jardine[1] demonstrated how companies were attempting to catch the eye in a variety of ways, especially when advertising in black and white **ILLUSTRATION 28**. Player's employed the cartoonist Archie White[2] in the middle of the decade to produce a series of advertisements that

1 Alex Jardine 1913–1987, painter and draughtsman, trained at St Martin's School of Art, specialised in book covers and wildlife art.

2 Archie White 1899–1957, cartoonist and watercolourist, trained at Central School of Arts and Crafts.

ILLUSTRATION 29

Punch, 1935

Watch out for the signs of jangled nerves

You've noticed other people's nervous habits—and wondered probably why such people didn't learn to control themselves.

But have you ever stopped to think that *you*, too, may have habits that are just as irritating to other people as those of the key juggler or coin jingler are to you?

And more important than that, those habits are a sign of jangled nerves. And jangled nerves are the signal to stop and check up on yourself.

Get enough sleep—fresh air—recreation—and watch your smoking.

Remember, you can smoke as many Camels as you want. Their costlier tobaccos *never* jangle the nerves.

COSTLIER TOBACCOS

Camels are made from finer, MORE EXPENSIVE TOBACCOS than any other popular brand.

How are YOUR *nerves?*
THIS *FREE* BOOK WILL TELL YOU

Shows 20 ways to test nerves—all illustrated. Instructive and amusing! Try them on your friends — see if *you* have healthy nerves yourself... Mail order-blank below with fronts from 2 packs of Camels. Free book comes postpaid.

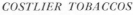

CLIP AND MAIL TODAY!

R. J. Reynolds Tobacco Company
Dept. 88-A, Winston-Salem, N. C.

I enclose fronts from 2 packs of Camels.
Send me book of nerve tests postpaid.

Name ....
(Print Name)

Street ....

City .... State ....
Offer expires December 31, 1934

CAMELS

SMOKE AS MANY AS YOU WANT
...THEY NEVER GET ON YOUR NERVES

ILLUSTRATION 30

Esquire, USA, 1934

a big
cocktail party—
a
hurried "hullo darling"—
and you're left
with a hitherto
strange young man . . .

have you
ever noticed
what
a
blessing
a
cigarette
can
be . . .

on occasions
such as this
when
you're
feeling
a
little
bit
" lost " ?

this is an advertisement depicting yet another occasion when Player's Cigarettes are welcome.

ILLUSTRATION 31

The Sketch, 1937

represented typical scenes from British social life. The illustrations were full of detail and packed with characters and incident. The idea was that the viewer was drawn into looking at the illustration for a long period and this would make the Player's brand even more familiar **ILLUSTRATION 29**. Player's was overtaking Wills's as the most popular brand in the UK at this time.

During the 1930s, advertisers recognised how many smokers used cigarettes as a way of reducing feelings of anxiety or tension. Many doctors would recommend smoking to relieve stress. Advertisements would acknowledge this health 'benefit' such as the Camel advertisement from 1934 **ILLUSTRATION 30** and one from a series for Player's which depicted people in awkward social situations being saved by offering or lighting up a cigarette **ILLUSTRATION 31**. Using cigarettes in social situations in this way was often an imitation of how smoking was portrayed in the cinema; cigarette smoking was equated with sex appeal and seduction. It has been calculated that about 30 per cent of the female Hollywood-based film heroines in the 1930s smoked, compared to only 2.5 per cent of female villains (Ernster, 1985, p.337). Smoking was being glamorised and links between smoking and beauty reinforced **ILLUSTRATION 32**.

Women were further encouraged to smoke as brands were produced intended to attract the female market. Some manufacturers produced smaller, slimmer and

CRAVEN "A"

Will not affect your throat

ILLUSTRATION 32

The Illustrated London News, 1939

more 'ladylike' cigarettes, others added cork tips to reduce strength and there were some that even had red tips to hide lipstick marks. Marlboro was originally produced by Philip Morris as a woman's cigarette. They were advertised as being 'Mild as May' for the female palate and had 'Ivory Tips' to 'protect the lips' **ILLUSTRATION 33** – quite a different image from the masculine symbol it was to become. In 1939 Philip Morris

sponsored a lecture tour in America, giving women lessons in cigarette smoking etiquette. Training was given in how to open packages and the proper ways to light, hold and extinguish cigarettes. Cigarette smoking was certainly not only respectable but desirable; Eleanor Roosevelt was smoking in public and even children were used to encourage their mothers to smoke **ILLUSTRATION 34**.

ILLUSTRATION 33

Esquire, USA, 1938

ILLUSTRATION 34

Punch, 1934

Mummy's Favourite

Mummy's favourite

This cheery little fellow on the cushion; always up to some mischief . . . . . At last he's captured a friendly rival . . . . . Another "Mummy's Favourite," one which also never loses its charm. And a *dependable* favourite which always soothes and brings content.

The fine flavour and cool smoking qualities of Player's Navy Cut Cork Tipped have made them the ladies' favourite Cigarette, the Cork Tip affording that smoothness and protection to the lips so often preferred.

PLAYER'S
NAVY CUT
10 FOR 6ᵈ CORK TIPPED CIGARETTES 20 FOR 11½ᵈ

Issued by The Imperial Tobacco Co. (of Great Britain and Ireland), Ltd.

NCC 157.

Chapter 4

1940s

Patriotism
and seduction

During the Second World War, the style of tobacco advertising changed. The link between smoking and patriotism that had been established in World War One was reinforced and developed. This State Express 555 advertisement from 1942 echoes similar patriotic and masculine images from World War One **ILLUSTRATION 35**. In Britain and America, cigarettes were declared as necessary as food and were also rationed in the same way. In 1941, Roosevelt relieved US tobacco farmers of military service as tobacco was declared an essential crop. Lucky Strike changed its packaging colours from dark green to white in 1942. The accompanying advertising campaign, 'Lucky Strike Green has gone to war' claimed that the change was made because the copper used in the green colour was required for the war effort. In fact, the change was more likely to have been a cost-cutting measure, but demonstrates how manufacturers were quick to link their products with patriotism. As during World War One, companies encouraged people to donate to 'tobacco funds' in order to ensure that members of the armed forces overseas would always be 'well supplied'. And well-supplied they were, as the twelve million strong US military machine were given free cigarettes as part of their combat ration. Thus the war guaranteed an expanded future customer base as millions of previously non-smoking young men and women sampled the product and became regular smokers. Additionally, American soldiers gave out their cigarettes to civilians as they moved through war-torn

Britain delivers the Goods
STATE EXPRESS
555

THE BEST CIGARETTES IN THE WORLD

EXPORT PACKING

ILLUSTRATION 35

Punch's Almanack, 1942

The American-born Duchess of Windsor presides in person at the United Services Canteen in the beautiful old Bahamian Club in Nassau. She takes an active part in making her service guests feel at home—cooks eggs and bacon, carries trays and hands out cigarettes.

IN NASSAU AT THE *Duchess of Windsor's*

UNITED SERVICES CANTEEN WHERE OUR SOLDIERS AND OUR ALLIES MEET

Chesterfield
is the Smoker's Choice

Yes, and it's Chesterfield at canteens, ship stores, post exchanges and everywhere that smokers want a milder, better-tasting smoke.

The basic difference between Chesterfield and other cigarettes is in the tobaccos we use and the way they are blended in the *right combination* to give you what you want in a smoke. They really SATISFY.

Copyright 1943, LIGGETT & MYERS TOBACCO CO.

GOVERNMENT HOUSE
NASSAU

June 17, 1943

Liggett & Myers Tobacco Co.,
630 Fifth Avenue,
New York, N. Y.

Dear Sirs:
Answering your inquiry as to what cigarettes we have here at the Canteen, I can say that we carry all the leading American brands.
Our records show that day in and day out smokers show a preference for Chesterfield over all other brands by a margin of four to one.
Of course, most of the Service men who come to the Canteen are British and American, but there are representatives of all the other Allied Nations.
It never occurred to me to ask any of the men why they preferred Chesterfields, but it's quite evident that Chesterfields are what 80% of them want.
Sincerely,
Wallis Windsor

ILLUSTRATION 36
1943

Women in the War

In this photo the Motor Corps of the American Women's Voluntary Services is represented. The young lady standing is dressed for duty behind the wheel. Blue-gray tunic, skirt, visored cap, dispatch case, brown leather belt. The seated driver wears her working uniform for *under* a car. The Camels are an important part of the uniform, too. The same grand flavor and extra mildness that make them such a favorite with men in uniform click with women in uniform, too.

The trim, alert drivers of the British-American Ambulance Corps look very smart in their blue-gray "R.A.F. style" uniforms. These girls can read a map like a field marshal, drive in the pitch darkness of a black-out, assemble a motor, do a man's work any day. Steady nerves are a must on a job like theirs. Notice how many of them smoke Camels. And remember, Camels are the favorite with the men in the armed forces.

Wherever you find the Services you find Camels

Steady Nerves ...that's the order of the hour not only with the *men* in all the armed services but in all the *women's* services, too.

Here is a member of The National Security Women's Corps. An ambitious recruit, having passed her courses, is entitled to wear this smart uniform of slate blue with brown belt and overseas cap. Motor mechanics, rifle shooting, map reading, hospital aid, fire wardening are just a few of the courses studied. The cigarette — Camel, of course. Camels are a favorite in the services.

This crisp, efficient-looking young lady is dressed for service as a Hospital Aide in the American Women's Hospitals Reserve Corps. You see Camels everywhere in the women's services. "They're so mild. And they taste so good," women say. You hear that all over.

CAMEL
TURKISH & DOMESTIC BLEND CIGARETTES
CHOICE QUALITY

R. J. Reynolds Tobacco Company
Winston-Salem, North Carolina

For Steady Pleasure

Camels

FIRST IN THE SERVICES
In the Army, Navy, Marines, Coast Guard the Favorite Cigarette is Camel
(BASED ON ACTUAL SALES RECORDS IN POST EX-CHANGES, SALES COMMISSARIES, SHIP'S SERVICE STORES, SHIP'S STORES, AND CANTEENS)

ILLUSTRATION 37

1942

ILLUSTRATION 38

1948

ILLUSTRATION 39
Saturday Evening Post, USA, 1946

regions, thereby creating an alternative currency in the barter economy, and developing a taste for American blended tobacco that the tobacco companies would learn to exploit in the post-war period (Kluger, 1996, p.113). The advertisement for Chesterfield cigarettes cleverly linked the brand not only with assisting the war effort, but also associated it with the glamorous Duchess of Windsor **ILLUSTRATION 36**.

These links between smoking and patriotism overshadowed any remaining moral objections to women smoking cigarettes. By this time, about one-third of American women smoked. Magazine advertisements portrayed women who smoked as role models who worked hard for the national effort. An American Camel advertisement from 1942 **ILLUSTRATION 37** epitomises this image of the independent woman taking on the same responsibilities as men. Interestingly, after the war,

the emphasis changed in cigarette advertising. Women were once more shown in traditional roles, as wives enjoying reunions with returning husbands or as brides taking cartons of cigarettes on their honeymoons (Ernster, 1985, p.337).

As women were once more portrayed in the domestic role, smoking continued to be linked with masculinity in advertising. Capstan used an image of a masculine, burly sailor in its post-war campaign **ILLUSTRATION 38** and most images of the ideal nuclear family had two children (one boy and one girl), an adoring mother and a pipe-smoking father such as in this illustration used in an advertisement for a major American industrial company **ILLUSTRATION 39**. Pipe smoking was associated with success and maturity, rather than the more youthful, sexual and active image of the cigarette smoker. These distinctions continued long into the 1950s and even 1960s.

ILLUSTRATION 40

1942

RITA HAYWORTH
Columbia Pictures Star
with her own Chesterfield
vanity-cigarette case

IN MY CASE *It's*
Chesterfield

In mine too say millions of satisfied
smokers . . . for a *Milder* and *decidedly Better-Tasting*
cigarette, one that's *Cooler-Smoking*, you just naturally
pick Chesterfield.

And of course the big thing in Chesterfield that
is giving everybody so much more smoking pleasure
is its Right Combination of the world's best cigarette
tobaccos . . . *for regardless of price there is no better
cigarette made today.*

MAKE YOUR NEXT PACK CHESTERFIELDS . . . *and enjoy 'em* *They Satisfy*

ILLUSTRATION 41

Punch, 1944

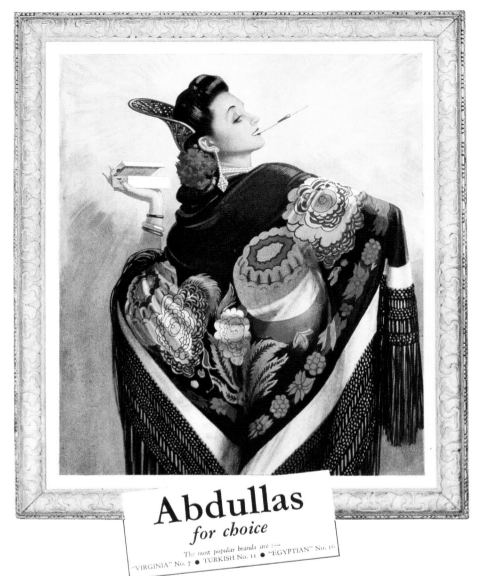

Abdullas
for choice

The most popular brands are :—
"VIRGINIA" No. 7 ● TURKISH No. 11 ● "EGYPTIAN" No. 16

The cinema continued to reinforce the cultural ubiquity of smoking. Screen actors used cigarettes in a multitude of different ways to portray fear, nervousness, dominance, control or sexuality. In *Now Voyager*, Paul Henreid created a smoking cliché as he lit two cigarettes in his mouth and handed one to that prototypical female screen smoker, Bette Davis. Hollywood stars continued to endorse smoking in advertising too. A Chesterfield advertisement from 1942 shows the reflected image of Rita Hayworth in the lid of a stylish cigarette case **ILLUSTRATION 40**. Abdullas continued to advance the glamorous and exotic image of cigarette smoking with this illustrated advertisement **ILLUSTRATION 41**.

ILLUSTRATION 42

Saturday Evening Post,
USA, 1946

THE SATURDAY EVENING POST

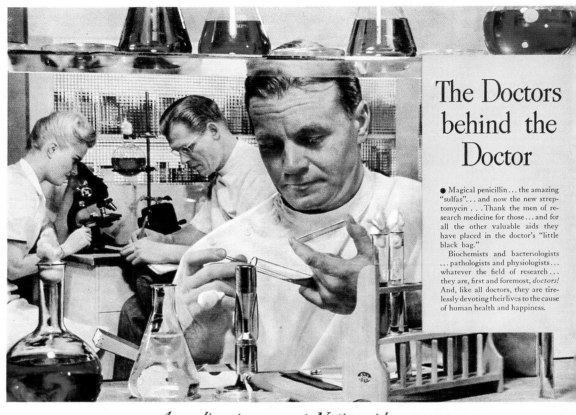

The Doctors behind the Doctor

● Magical penicillin... the amazing "sulfas"... and now the new streptomycin ... Thank the men of research medicine for those... and for all the other valuable aids they have placed in the doctor's "little black bag."

Biochemists and bacteriologists ... pathologists and physiologists... whatever the field of research ... they are, first and foremost, *doctors!* And, like all doctors, they are tirelessly devoting their lives to the cause of human health and happiness.

According to a recent Nationwide survey:

MORE DOCTORS SMOKE CAMELS THAN ANY OTHER CIGARETTE

● What cigarette do you smoke, Doctor?...that was the question put up to 113,597 doctors from the Atlantic to the Pacific, from the Gulf of Mexico to the Canadian border. Three independent research organizations did the asking ...covered doctors in every branch of medicine.
The brand named most was Camel!
Like the rest of us, doctors smoke for pleasure. Their taste recognizes and appreciates the rich, full flavor and cool mildness of Camel's costlier tobaccos just as yours does.

YOUR "T-ZONE" WILL TELL YOU...

T for Taste ...
T for Throat ...

that's your proving ground for any cigarette. See if Camels don't suit your "T-Zone" to a "T."

CAMELS *Costlier Tobaccos*

TURKISH & DOMESTIC BLEND CIGARETTES

CHOICE QUALITY

R. J. Reynolds
Tobacco Company
Winston-Salem

Throughout the 1940s, no significant evidence was produced relating to the health risks of tobacco. Despite the fact that lung cancer had increased at five times the rate of other forms of cancer between 1938 and 1948 in America, the link with smoking was still not being made. Cigarette smoke was generally understood to contain irritants and toxins that were low level and slow acting. These moderate health concerns were addressed by the tobacco companies, assuring consumers in their advertisements that their products were less harmful than others and sometimes even implying that they were beneficial. Camel claimed in a 1946 American advertisement **ILLUSTRATION 42** that more doctors smoke their brand, implying that if a doctor makes that choice, it must mean that the product is good for you. Philip Morris's claims for lower throat irritation, as illustrated by an advertisement from 1943 **ILLUSTRATION 43**, were challenged by the Federal Trade Commission, but the matter was not resolved until 1955, by which time the company had long since dropped its health claim (Kluger, 1996, pp.131–132).

ILLUSTRATION 43
1943

MEDICAL AUTHORITIES
RECOGNIZE
PHILIP MORRIS
proved far less irritating to the smoker's nose and throat!

WHEN SMOKERS CHANGED TO PHILIP MORRIS, EVERY CASE OF IRRITATION OF NOSE OR THROAT — DUE TO SMOKING — EITHER CLEARED COMPLETELY OR DEFINITELY IMPROVED!

—facts reported in medical journals, on clinical tests made by distinguished doctors. Proof that this better-tasting cigarette is better for you . . . less irritant to nose and throat!

CALL FOR
PHILIP MORRIS
America's Finest Cigarette

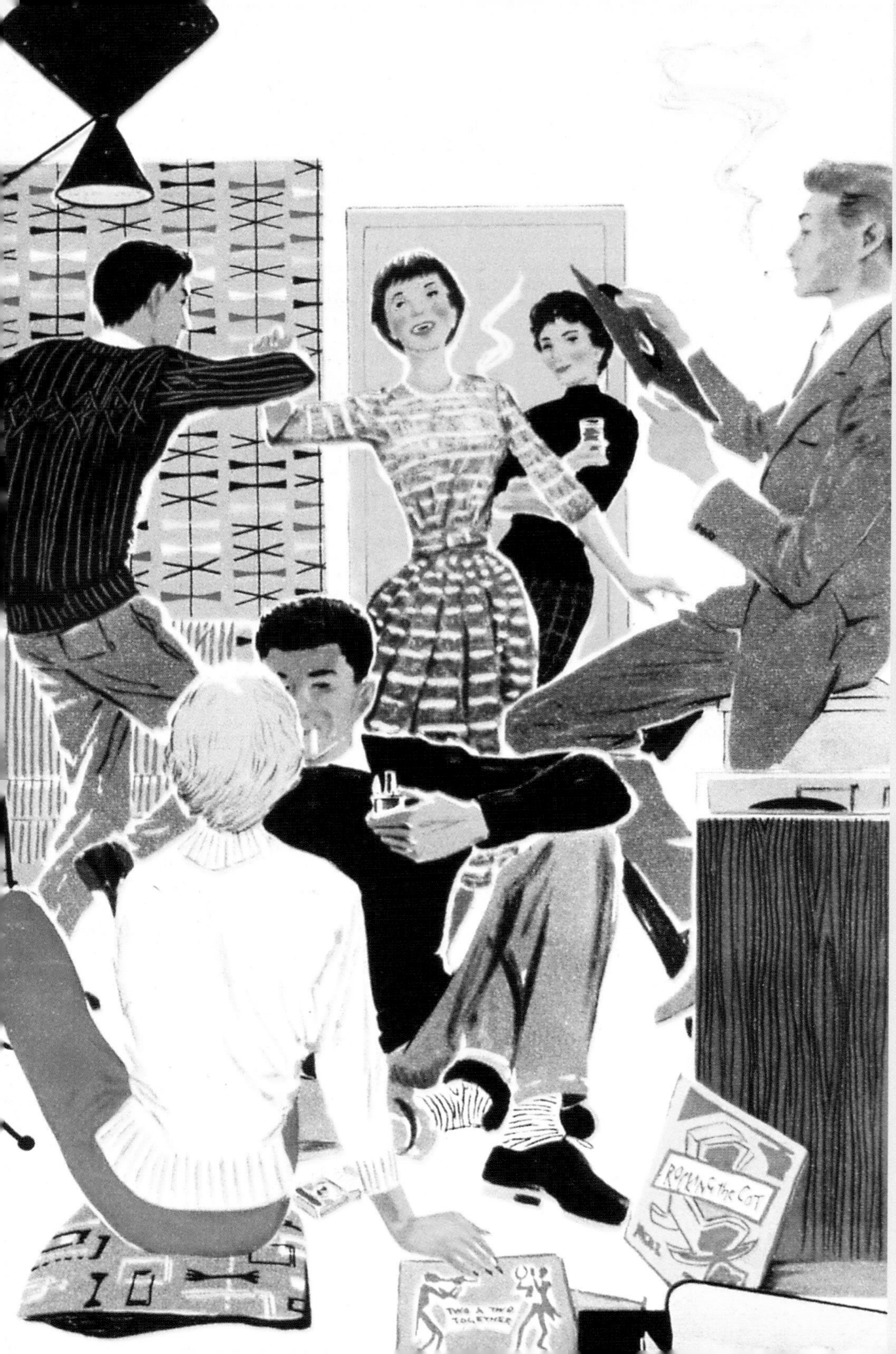

Chapter 5

1950s

Smokers' cough

n 1950, Richard Doll and A Bradford Hill published a preliminary report in the *British Medical Journal* on the link between smoking and lung cancer. Their conclusion was that 'smoking is a factor, and an important factor, in the production of carcinoma of the lung' (Doll and Hill, 1950, p.746). Other medical researchers were beginning to investigate the health risks of smoking and articles and letters appeared regularly in the medical press in both the United States and Britain during the 1950s. By the end of the decade, the causal connection between smoking and lung cancer was generally accepted by the medical community. Governments were slow to respond and instigate public health education and awareness campaigns, despite lobbying from influential medics, until the mid-1960s. Old Gold seemed more than aware of the risks that tobacco companies took in claiming the health benefits of smoking in a peculiar advertisement of 1950 ILLUSTRATION 44. This advertisement seemed to mark a conscious decision that cigarette manufacturers were being forced to make at this time, to focus consumers on the 'pleasure' of smoking and to negate any implied connection with health issues.

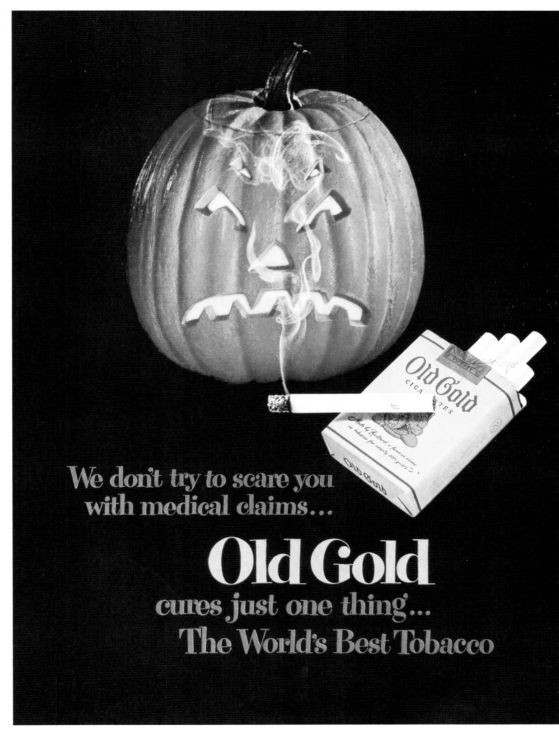

We don't try to scare you
with medical claims…

Old Gold

cures just one thing…
The World's Best Tobacco

ILLUSTRATION 45

John Bull, 1953

Tobacco companies attempted to counter the negative effects of the health implications by introducing filters into their products and by shifting the emphasis in their advertising to associating smoking with fitness, pleasure and the outdoor life. They used sport personalities to promote their products. The Craven 'A' endorsement from the famous football player Sir Stanley Matthews in 1953 ILLUSTRATION 45 suggested that smoking was no handicap to sporting achievement and a healthy lifestyle. A Player's Navy Cut advertisement from 1954 not only suggested the 'postcoital' cigarette but placed the smokers in an idyllic countryside environment ILLUSTRATION 46. The emphasis was on sexual pleasure and relaxation with no health associations. Capstan shifted its angle in a pretty advertisement from 1951, promoting the sociability of smoking and the suggestion that non-smokers don't fit in ILLUSTRATION 47.

ILLUSTRATION 46

Picture Post, 1954

Whatever the pleasure
Player's complete it

IT'S THE TOBACCO THAT COUNTS

(NCC 864)

ILLUSTRATION 47

1951

Made by W. D. & H. O. Wills, Branch of The Imperial Tobacco Co. (of Great Britain & Ireland), Ltd.

CC 748 J.

ILLUSTRATION 48
1957

Whatever the pleasure
Player's complete it

Player's Please

Now Millions Know! **ONE**

KING SIZE

tops 'em all for TASTE and COMFORT!

Your throat can tell—
it's PHILIP MORRIS

LUCILLE BALL
starring in the
Lucille Ball, Desi Arnaz
"I LOVE LUCY" Show
CBS-TV

No matter what brand you're now smoking . . . there's greater pleasure waiting for you in the new PHILIP MORRIS King-Size. Millions of smokers who tried them are buying them over and over again! Once you try them, you will, too. Because *your throat can tell* that here, at last, is a cigarette not only good to *smoke* . . . but good to the *smoker* . . . good to *you!* Try a carton—*now!*

KING-SIZE

REGULAR

CALL FOR **PHILIP MORRIS**

ILLUSTRATION 49
1953

ILLUSTRATION 50

1944

Cigarette of successful men and lovely women

The portrayal of smoking as a leisure activity to be enjoyed in a group is consistently reinforced by advertising during the 1950s. A Player's advertisement from 1957 directly appealed to the new youth market ILLUSTRATION 51. Note the distinctive contemporary fabric and fashion designs that defined the period.

Cigarette advertisements were not as prominent in the printed media during this decade because of the development and success of advertising on television. Celebrity endorsements continued to be used successfully, but the stars were more likely to be of the small screen rather than the cinema. A Philip Morris advertisement from 1953 used the recommendation of Lucille Ball, a huge television star in both America and Britain ILLUSTRATION 49.

Perhaps the most famous and successful advertising campaign of all was launched in the 1950s. As has been mentioned, Marlboro had been launched in 1924 as a woman's cigarette. The advertisement from 1944 ILLUSTRATION 50 shows Philip Morris was marketing the cigarette to the luxury market, especially to women, to justify its higher price. Even in 1951, Philip Morris was using this particularly strange image of an adorable infant with a baby-pink background ILLUSTRATION 48 to sell cigarettes to mothers. According to Philip Morris's research, many smokers regarded filter cigarettes as effeminate and 'sissy', so the company was determined to create and market a filter cigarette which was as

masculine as possible. The early 'new' Marlboro advertisements in 1954 pictured images of men who typified 'masculine confidence'. Sometimes an image of a cowboy was used as the 'most generally accepted symbol of masculinity in America' (Burnett, 1958, p.42). In order to further enhance the macho and mystery of the male smoker, a tattoo was inscribed on the hand of the model in the advertisement. In later advertisements the face of the model was removed, and only the torso and the tattooed hand were shown, as in an example from 1958 ILLUSTRATION 51. The message of machismo was reinforced visually by the adoring look of the woman in the background and the text 'where there's a Man… there's a Marlboro'. Later the campaign was refined by the Leo Burnett advertising agency to the image that was to endure all over the world for the next thirty years, the Marlboro cowboy and 'Marlboro Country'. By 1972, Marlboro had become the best-selling cigarette in the world.

ILLUSTRATION 51
Saturday Evening Post, USA, 1951

Where there's a Man...

The cigarette designed for men that women like

there's a Marlboro

The Marlboro Filter. Cellulose acetate is the modern effective filter material for cigarettes. This unretouched photo shows the cellulose acetate in just one Marlboro exclusive Selectrate Filter.

—with a filter that delivers a smoke of surprising mildness

YOU GET A LOT TO LIKE... FILTER, FLAVOR, FLIP-TOP BOX

(From a prized recipe of the world's great tobaccos)

Sturdiest box of all— with exclusive self-starter

ILLUSTRATION 52

1958

Chapter 6

1960s

The 'New Way'

The 1960s saw the reinforcement of the Marlboro cowboy in American and international popular culture **ILLUSTRATION 53**. After 1964 when the 'Marlboro Country' campaign was established, sales of Marlboro increased by an average of 10 per cent each year. Other brands took up this successful approach by changing their tactics to the enhancement of personal image. This worked well, especially for men, whose consumption of cigarettes had been in decline since the 1950s. A Lucky Strike advertisement from 1964, blatantly exploits the manly associations of firearms, even underlining the word 'Man' for additional emphasis **ILLUSTRATION 54**. In Britain, a stylishly directed campaign for Bachelor cigarettes by Player's, was also directed at the male smoker and pictured the silhouette of a man in profile with only the open packet of cigarettes visible in a pool of light **ILLUSTRATION 55**.

You get a lot to like with a Marlboro—filter, flavor, pack or box.

Come to where the flavor is. Come to Marlboro Country.

ILLUSTRATION 53

1966

GIVE
A MAN
A LUCKY

**LUCKY
STRIKE**
IT'S TOASTED

CIGARETTES

MADE IN U.S.A.

Man-size flavor…man-size satisfaction…that's Lucky Strike!

ILLUSTRATION 54

Life International, 1969

ILLUSTRATION 55
Punch, 1962

Punch, March 14 1962

The
tip
that's
setting
the
trend

ILLUSTRATION 56

The Illustrated London News, 1964

...and with cigarettes too, there's the new way It's typical of Britain to welcome the best of the new and conserve the best of the old...and Rothmans King Size are the new way in cigarettes, part of the changing face of Britain today. Rothmans, the first King Size in Britain and the world, give you extra length, a finer filter and the best tobacco money can buy. Twenty for 4/6. **Rothmans King Size—smooth, really satisfies**

The style of advertising was changing in the 1960s. A Rothmans advertisement of 1964 reflects the building and architectural boom of this period in Britain when roads, tower blocks and the growth of the modern skyline exemplified the 'new way' depicted in the image **ILLUSTRATION 56**. The free brush and mixed media styles of new artists such as Robert Rauchenberg and early David Hockney, seem to have influenced the design of Peter Stuyvesant advertisements from 1964 **ILLUSTRATION 57**. Companies were becoming more adventurous in embracing influences from the art world.

ILLUSTRATION 57

The Illustrated London News, 1964

Back in 1910 Mrs. Mullins never understood why her husband wouldn't let her smoke. Mr. Mullins never understood why his wife wouldn't let him install indoor plumbing.

You've come a long way, baby.

VIRGINIA SLIMS

With rich Virginia flavor women like.

Regular: 16 mg.'tar,'' 1.0 mg. nicotine—Menthol: 15 mg.''tar,'' 1.0 mg. nicotine av. per cigarette, FTC Report Oct.'74

Warning: The Surgeon General Has Determined That Cigarette Smoking Is Dangerous to Your Health

In 1915, Mrs. Cheryl Van Eaton cleverly hid her cigarettes in a hollow duck decoy. The decoy fooled her husband and 750 southbound mallards.

You've come a long way, b

VIRGINIA SLIMS

With rich Virginia flavor women li

Regular: 17 mg.'tar,'' 1.0 mg. nicotine—Menthol: 17 mg.'' tar,'' 1.1 mg. nicotine av. per cigarette, FTC Re

Warning: The Surgeon General Has Determined That Cigarette Smoking Is Dangerous to Your Health.

ILLUSTRATION 58

1978

As the evidence linking smoking with fatal diseases grew, calls came to restrict advertising. In 1962, the Royal College of Physicians highlighted the problems and recommended stricter laws on the sale and advertising of tobacco products. In 1965 in Britain, a ban was placed on all television commercials for cigarettes, but commercials for loose tobacco and cigars continued until 1991. Also in 1965, new legislation in America led to the appearance of the following health warning on all packets of cigarettes, 'Caution – Cigarette Smoking May Be Hazardous to Your Health'.

Although the number of male smokers was in decline (in Britain, male smoking rates fell from 82 per cent to 38 per cent between 1948 and 1990 [Hilton, 2000, p.231]) the levels of female smokers remained steady into the

1960s. In America, about 33 per cent of women were smokers through this period. Manufacturers continued to attempt to attract women by using the significant changes in society such as the sexual liberation movement to associate smoking for women with independence, power and status. The Virginia Slims brand was introduced by Philip Morris in 1968, exploiting women's desire for social independence by portraying the contrast between contemporary 'liberated' women and the women of the past for whom it was not respectable to smoke. The advertisements emphasised the progress with the slogan 'You've come a long way, baby' **ILLUSTRATION 58**. This campaign continued until the late 1990s and within six years the percentage of teenage women who smoked had doubled (Kluger, 1996, p.317). Smoking had been successfully established as a symbol for women of independence and sexual liberation. An advertisement for Liggett & Myers clearly illustrates this change in sexual attitudes **ILLUSTRATION 59**. Women were less frequently shown in cigarette advertising as workers, housewives or mothers.

Should a nice girl go this far just for a cigarette?

ILLUSTRATION 59

1967

Chapter 7

1970s

Living with the bans

As the health risks of smoking were now accepted and acknowledged by governments, the 1970s saw a battle by the tobacco companies against restrictive legislation and the attempt to retain consumer levels. In 1971 in America, a ban was introduced on cigarette advertising on radio and television following the British example, and in Britain in the same year, the industry agreed to put health warnings on all packets and make reference to the health warnings on advertisements. Cigarette advertising lost some of its originality and inventiveness as the cautious companies sought to avoid government sanctions by ensuring that their advertising could not be seen to glamorise smoking. Advertisements for Embassy, Silk Cut and Player's Gold Leaf **ILLUSTRATIONS 60, 61, 62,** clearly illustrate how companies resorted to focusing advertising on brand and packet recognition. The images are nevertheless stylish and well produced.

Since the 1950s, strategies had been introduced by the tobacco companies to try to reverse a slow decline in smoking, especially among men. The inclusion of filters in cigarettes was now firmly established and each company was introducing 'low-tar' brands to smokers who were concerned about the health effects of smoking. This suggested that there was an alternative to giving up the habit all together. From 1970, American companies voluntarily agreed to display tar and nicotine data on cigarette packaging. From 1975 in Britain, the tobacco

LOW TAR As defined by H.M.Government
ERY PACKET CARRIES A GOVERNMENT HEALTH WARNING

ILLUSTRATION 60

The Illustrated London News, 1976

MIDDLE TAR
As defined in H.M.Government Tables published in February 1976.
EVERY PACKET CARRIES A GOVERNMENT HEALTH WARNING.

ILLUSTRATION 61

Telegraph Sunday Magazine, 1979

Enjoy the good taste

ILLUSTRATION 62
The Illustrated London News, 1973

EVERY PACKET CARRIES A GOVERNMENT HEALTH WARNING

EVERY PACKET CARRIES A GOVERNMENT HEALTH WARNING

ILLUSTRATION 63
1970s

Shoes by Yves St. Laurent. Cigarettes by John Player.

EVERY PACKET CARRIES A GOVERNMENT HEALTH WARNING

ILLUSTRATION 64
1974

companies and the government had come to an agreement that tobacco advertisements would no longer suggest that cigarettes were safe, popular or healthy and no link would be made between smoking and social, sexual or business success. Advertisements for Dunhill, Rothmans and John Player Special **ILLUSTRATIONS 63, 64, 65** from the early 1970s are examples of the kind of advertising that was no longer permitted after 1975.

ILLUSTRATION 65
1970

Let
him
light it
—but
this
one's
yours

LONG, RICH, MILD-TASTING

SLIM SIZE
BY
dunhill

5/5 for 20
Recommended Price

The most distinguished tobacco house in the world

After the ban on television and radio advertising, companies started to target women smokers again, particularly via printed advertising in women's magazines which had the highest circulation of all publications. An advertisement for Max cigarettes **ILLUSTRATION 66** illustrates the language companies used in their advertising directed at women and suggested the link between smoking and weight loss. Words such as 'thin', 'long', 'lean' and 'slim' were descriptions of the cigarettes themselves, but also implied that the product could be used as a slimming aid. Cigarette advertising was particularly prevalent in slimming magazines. Max advertisements bizarrely suggest that smoking longer cigarettes may reduce the health risks associated with smoking heavily.

ILLUSTRATION 66

Vogue, USA, 1976

You can smoke fewer cigarettes by smoking longer ones.

"It's wacky, but it works."

Max 120's.

Long, lean, delicious.
They take longer to
smoke so you don't
light up as often.

Regular: 17 mg. "tar,"
1.2 mg. nicotine; Menthol:
17 mg. "tar," 1.3 mg.
nicotine av. per cigarette
by FTC Report April 1976.

Warning: The Surgeon General Has Determined
That Cigarette Smoking Is Dangerous to Your Health.

U.S. Government figures show Pall Mall 100's now lower in "tar" than the best-selling filter king.

You make out better at both ends.
Longer – yet milder!

PALL MALL
100's
20 CIGARETTES
FAMOUS CIGARETTES
FILTER TIPPED

PALL MALL
20 CIGARETTES
FILTER CIGARETTES
MENTHOL

"How does that grab you?"

© The American Tobacco Company

ILLUSTRATION 67
1970

In addition to targeting women, American tobacco companies also noticed that people from ethnic and racial minorities generally smoked less than white people. A rise in the number of cigarette billboards in Black or Latino communities and specific targeting in magazines **ILLUSTRATION 67** resulted in a rise in the number of Afro-American smokers. Certain brands such as Dorado and L&M Supers were marketed specifically to the Hispanic market in the United States. Even the gay and lesbian communities have been targeted by the tobacco companies as a market with potential for growth. A Virginia Slims campaign focused on the lesbian community directly, using themes of liberation and individualism.

The world of
Lambert & Butler

Lambert and Butler
International Size, with a quality
and style that sets them apart
from other cigarettes.

LAMBERT & BUTLER
PARK LANE LONDON

MIDDLE TAR
As defined in H.M.Government Tables published in February 1976.
EVERY PACKET CARRIES A GOVERNMENT HEALTH WARNING.

In the mid-1970s in Britain, advertisers agreed that they would no longer depict people smoking in social situations in their advertisements. An advertisement from Lambert & Butler – note the distinctive 1970s décor and fashions – is one of the last examples of this kind of advertising **ILLUSTRATION 68**.

Chapter 8

Invention and
Inspiration

During the 1980s, governments were under increasing pressure to restrict tobacco advertising by legislation. During the decade discussions, deals and debates led to voluntary restrictions by the industry on tobacco advertising in order to forestall government decisions on legislation. In some ways, restrictions seemed to inspire the advertising agencies into creating some of the most inventive, striking and memorable advertising campaigns of the century.

The advertising agency Collett Dickenson Pearce started a campaign for Benson & Hedges in the mid-1970s that was to develop into a long-running classic. The surreal and high-quality photographic images focused on package recognition and challenged the viewer to interpret the visual clues, working on the theory that the more you are forced to use your imagination, the more you will remember. As veteran advertising professional John Hegarty[3] pointed out, 'ironically, sometimes the only words on the Benson & Hedges advertisements tell you not to smoke!' (Hegarty, 1998, p.224) An advertisement from 1974 ILLUSTRATION 69 was part of B&H's 'Pure Gold' campaign when they bravely excluded even an image of the packet from the picture. In many of their advertisements, the viewer's first clue that the advertisement was for cigarettes was from the government health warning. Advertisers were using the health warning to their advantage. The inventiveness of the B&H campaign continued into the 1980s with this

3 John Hegarty, b.1944, co-founder, Chairman and Worldwide Creative Director of BartleBogleHegarty, advertising agency.

Also available in a flip-top pack.

ILLUSTRATION 69

1974

EVERY PACKET CARRIES A GOVERNMENT HEALTH WARNING

ILLUSTRATION 70

The Illustrated London News, 1982

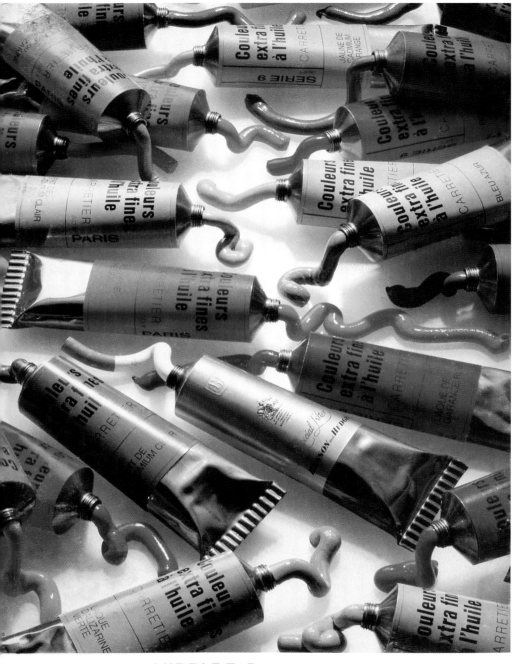

MIDDLE TAR As defined by H.M. Government
DANGER: H.M. Government Health Departments' WARNING:
THINK ABOUT THE HEALTH RISKS BEFORE SMOKING

ILLUSTRATION 71

Sunday Times Magazine, 1984

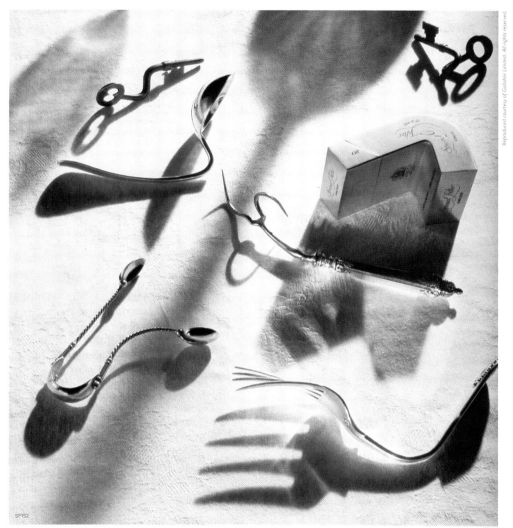

SF152

MIDDLE TAR As defined by H.M. Government
DANGER: Government Health WARNING:
CIGARETTES CAN SERIOUSLY DAMAGE YOUR HEALTH

eye-catching image from 1982 with an unexpected extrusion of a cigarette from a paint tube ILLUSTRATION 70. In 1984, the campaign exploited the national interest in the phenomenon of spoon bending as made famous by Uri Geller ILLUSTRATION 71. By the end of the decade, the advertisements represent practically nothing of the cigarette pack, but the product is still immediately recognisable ILLUSTRATION 72.

ILLUSTRATION 72

1988

MIDDLE TAR As defined by H.M. Government
DANGER: Government Health WARNING: CIGARETTES CAN SERIOUSLY DAMAGE YOUR HEALTH

CIGARETTES CAN SERIOUSLY DAMAGE YOUR HEALTH

ILLUSTRATION 73

Sunday Times Magazine, 1984

In 1986, advertisers were coming under stricter guidelines and in particular were no longer allowed to show a person smoking or even the image of a cigarette. In 1984, Saatchi & Saatchi predicted these particular restrictions on tobacco advertising and started a campaign for Silk Cut which was to result in the brand becoming the best-selling cigarette in Britain in the 1990s. The first advertisement in the campaign was the image of a length of purple silk with a knife slash through it ILLUSTRATION 73. The image said 'silk cut', but as a visual pun. Throughout the campaign, this play on the Silk Cut name was combined with the purple and white colours of the brand packaging. As the campaign developed, the agency created a kaleidoscope of inventive images such as a shark's fin in 1987 ILLUSTRATION 74 and a sinister representation of barbed wire in 1990 ILLUSTRATION 75. In none of these advertisements was the product or even the package required to be shown in order to attract the public's attention.

ILLUSTRATION 74
You magazine, 1987

LOW TAR As defined by H.M. Government
STOPPING SMOKING REDUCES THE RISK
OF SERIOUS DISEASES

LOW T

ILLUSTRATION 75

House & Garden, 1990

d by H.M. Government Warning: SMOKING CAN CAUSE FATAL DISEASES Health Departments' Chief Medical Officers

We're not allowed to tell you anything about Winston cigarettes, so here's a wok in the Black Forest.

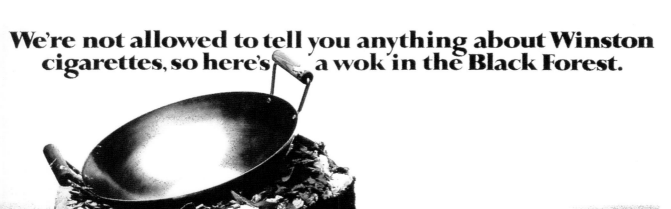

LOW TO MIDDLE TAR As defined by H.M.Government
DANGER: Government Health WARNING:CIGARETTES CAN SERIOUSLY DAMAGE YOUR HEALTH

ILLUSTRATION 76

1984

We're not allowed to tell you anything about Winston cigarettes, so here's a tart leaning on a bar.

ILLUSTRATION 77

Weekend, UK, 1984

LOW TO MIDDLE TAR As defined by H.M.Government
DANGER: Government Health WARNING:
CIGARETTES CAN SERIOUSLY DAMAGE YOUR HEALTH

ILLUSTRATION 78
1986

Dunhill King Size.

LOW TO MIDDLE TAR As defined by H.M. Government
DANGER: Government Health WARNING:
CIGARETTES CAN SERIOUSLY DAMAGE YOUR HEALTH

Winston confronted the problem of advertising restrictions head-on in its campaign devised by the J Walter Thompson agency. All the advertisements began with the line 'We're not allowed to tell you anything about Winston cigarettes, so here's….' and a visual pun would follow. These examples illustrate how the company was cleverly mocking the restrictions while still attracting attention and challenging the viewer ILLUSTRATIONS 76, 77. Many advertisers facing the same problems attempted to follow suit with varying degrees of success. Dunhill's attempt at imitating the successful surreal images of B&H and Silk Cut was not memorable ILLUSTRATION 78 but

Black in town

MIDDLE TAR As defined by H. M. Government
DANGER: Government Health WARNING:
CIGARETTES CAN SERIOUSLY DAMAGE YOUR HEALTH

ILLUSTRATION 79

1984

Black on the map

John Player Special

MIDDLE TAR Manufacturer's estimate.
DANGER: H.M. Government Health Departments' WARNI
THINK ABOUT THE HEALTH RISKS BEFORE SMOKI

ILLUSTRATION 80

1984

CAMEL

CAMEL
FILTERS

SMOOTH
TURKISH & DOMESTIC
BLEND

SURGEON GENERAL'S WARNING: Smoking
Causes Lung Cancer, Heart Disease,
Emphysema, And May Complicate Pregnancy.

17 mg. "tar", 1.1 mg. nicotine av. per cigarette by FTC method.

ILLUSTRATION 81

Rolling Stone, USA, 1990

John Player Special ran a long and successful campaign using the package colour of its branding and verbal play on the word 'black' ILLUSTRATIONS 79, 80.

Tobacco companies in America were not experiencing the same restrictions on their advertising during the 1980s and 1990s as in Britain. They were focusing campaigns on women and minority communities as has been noted in chapter 7. The Camel campaign launched in 1988 was an example of the tobacco industry targeting the youth market. The campaign featured a cartoon camel known as 'Joe Camel' and according to research in 1991, more children aged five and six could recognise Joe Camel than could recognise Mickey Mouse (Fisher, Schwartz et al, 1991, p.266). RJ Reynolds, the company behind the Camel brand, denied that Joe Camel was intended to be directed at children, but in 1997 it finally ceased to use the character in its campaigns under pressure from Congress and public interest groups ILLUSTRATION 81.

During this period, tobacco companies were looking for alternative ways of promoting their products, realising that direct advertising would soon be further restricted

LOW TO MIDDLE TAR Manufacturer's estimate

DANGER: H.M. Government Health Departments' WARNING THINK ABOUT THE HEALTH RISKS BEFORE SMOKING.

ILLUSTRATION 82

Sunday Times Magazine, 1982

by most Western governments. Tobacco sponsorship of sports was to become a very popular method of promoting tobacco products. In the early 1980s, tobacco companies were starting to sponsor sporting events to help associate their products with physical achievement and competition. There was some controversy in 1982 when Martina Navratilova won the Wimbledon tennis tournament wearing an outfit bearing the Kim cigarette brand colours of brown, yellow and orange. Kim was a British American Tobacco brand that was established as a women's cigarette. The Dorland advertising agency

developed a campaign which projected the brand's feminine appeal by using graphic female symbols like umbrellas, high-heeled shoes or cocktail glasses, all in the distinctive brand colours ILLUSTRATION 82. Sports sponsorship continued to be a successful promotional avenue for tobacco companies and by the early twenty-first century it was estimated that tobacco companies in the UK spent around eight million pounds on sports sponsorship and around seventy million pounds on Formula One sponsorship which associated their brand with excitement and glamour.

ILLUSTRATION 83

Health Education Council, 1980s

If only.

Nobody has ever smoked an entire cigarette.

In fact, about two-thirds of the smoke produced by a cigarette goes straight into the atmosphere.

Which in a room, pub, restaurant or cinema can create an extremely unpleasant atmosphere.

Breathing other people's cigarette smoke doesn't just get up non-smokers' noses.

It gets down their throats and into their lungs.

According to the British Medical Journal (and we quote) "substances released into the air from tobacco smoke can be assumed to cause at least some cases of lung cancer."

The article goes on to say that the children of parents who smoke have more chest infections than the children of non-smokers.

If you smoke, we hope you'll spare a thought for the majority who don't. And if you don't smoke, but live or work with people who do, we hope you'll put this advertisement where they can't miss it.

Right under their noses.

Don't force smoking down other people's throats.

FOR A FREE LEAFLET, 'BREATHING OTHER PEOPLE'S TOBACCO SMOKE', WRITE TO THE HEALTH EDUCATION COUNCIL, DEPT 682, 22-24 CLARKE ROAD, MOUNT FARM, MILTON KEYNES MK1 1LG

If You Smoke, You Might As Well Start The Day With A Mouthful Of This.

Minnesota Department of Health

ILLUSTRATION 84
Minnesota Department of Health, 1989

Because of the dangers of smoking and the increasing costs of treating smoking-related illnesses, governments attempted to counter the inventiveness and advertising resources of the tobacco companies with their own campaigns. Most used health scares or irony in order to persuade people to give up or not to start smoking. One famous advertisement had the text 'This table is reserved for smokers' above an image of a hospital gurney. Many campaigns have concentrated on the links with lung cancer and heart disease, others have attempted to highlight the problem of passive smoking, such as the clever image created for the Health Education Council in 1987 ILLUSTRATION 83. Other effective campaigns have drawn attention to the effect of smoking on bad breath and general attractiveness. The award-winning advertisement by the Minnesota Department of Health in 1991 ILLUSTRATION 84 certainly left a bad taste in the mouth, and the unattractive image for the American Cancer Society attempts to counter the decades of advertising that linked smoking with glamour ILLUSTRATION 85.

ILLUSTRATION 85
American Cancer Society, 1970s

As part of their 1997 election campaign, the Labour Party in Britain pledged to ban all advertising of tobacco products. This legislation came into effect in 2003 when all general advertising of tobacco and sports sponsorship was made illegal. In the United States however, tobacco companies spend around fifteen billion dollars on advertising each year. Tobacco is one of the most heavily marketed consumer products in America, second only to the automobile industry. Now ended in Britain and Europe, tobacco advertising continues in America; that surprisingly successful endeavour to draw us to buy a product that we all know to be addictive and possibly dangerous and deadly.

ABDULLA – a brand of cigarettes using Turkish tobacco which was acquired by Gallaher in 1961.

ARMY CLUB – a cigarette produced by Cavander's which was based in Glasgow, Scotland.

BACHELOR – a Player's brand, now owned by Imperial Tobacco.

BENSON & HEDGES – founded in 1873 by Richard Benson and William Hedges. Benson & Hedges was acquired by Gallaher in 1955 and now Gallaher makes B&H for the UK market while BAT is the manufacturer for international markets.

BLACK CAT – introduced by House of Carreras in 1904. From 1910, coupons were offered in the packets that could be traded for gifts. A very successful brand which then went into decline after World War II and was finally withdrawn in 1993. Trademark still owned by BAT.

BRITISH AMERICAN TOBACCO PLC (BAT) – established in 1902. A joint venture between Imperial Tobacco Co and American Tobacco Co.

CAMEL – introduced by American tobacco company RJ Reynolds in 1914.

CAPSTAN – a British cigarette originally made by Wills, now owned by Imperial Tobacco.

CHESTERFIELD – introduced by Liggett & Myers in 1912 as a Turkish–Virginia blended cigarette. It was named after Chesterfield County in Virginia. Using the Chesterfield brand, Liggett & Myers was the first to offer two sizes of cigarette, king size and regular in 1952. The Chesterfield brand was sold to Philip Morris (now Altria) in 1999.

CRAVEN 'A' – launched by House of Carreras in 1921. It was the first machine-made cigarette with a cork tip. Carreras was established by Don Jose Carreras Ferrer, a Spanish nobleman in the nineteenth century. The company merged with Rothmans in 1958.

DE RESZKE – a brand introduced by British company J Millhoff & Co.

DORADO – a brand established by Liggett & Myers in 1984 aimed at the American Hispanic market.

DU MAURIER – named after Sir Gerald du Maurier, a British actor and theatre manager who died in 1934. The brand is now owned by British American Tobacco.

DUNHILL – originally owned by Rothmans and then BAT.

Distributed in the USA by RJ Reynolds. Marketed as a luxury cigarette and more expensive than most other brands.

EMBASSY – a British brand now owned by Imperial Tobacco. First introduced by Wills in 1914 and then relaunched in 1962.

FATIMA – an American cigarette very popular at the beginning of the twentieth century. Created by Liggett & Myers, now owned by Philip Morris.

GALLAHER – an international company founded in 1857 by Thomas Gallaher in Northern Ireland.

HERBERT TAREYTON – a brand of cigarettes first manufactured by the American Tobacco Company and now owned by RJ Reynolds.

IMPERIAL TOBACCO GROUP PLC – a major international tobacco company based in Bristol, England. It was formed in 1901 from a merger of thirteen family-run businesses to resist competition from the United States. The first chairman was Sir William Henry Wills.

JOHN PLAYER SPECIAL – see Player's

KIM – a brand marketed to women in Europe by BAT's German company (BAT Cigaretten-Fabriken) since 1971.

LAMBERT & BUTLER – the UK's top selling brand, produced by Imperial Tobacco.

LIGGETT & MYERS (L&M) – established in 1822 by Christopher Foulks who opened a snuff shop in Illinois. L&M was sold to Philip Morris in 1999.

LORILLARD TOBACCO COMPANY – America's first tobacco company, founded in 1760 by entrepreneur Pierre Lorillard.

LUCKY STRIKE – introduced by R.A. Patterson of Richmond, Virginia in 1871 as a chewing tobacco and later as a cigarette. Acquired by American Tobacco Company in 1905 and now owned by RJ Reynolds.

MARLBORO – launched in 1924 by Philip Morris. Originally marketed as a women's cigarette and relaunched in 1954 with new packaging and associated masculine advertising campaign. By 1972 it was the best selling brand in the world and still the top selling brand in the USA in 2000.

MAX – an American brand introduced by Lorillard Tobacco Company.

MOGUL – an American cigarette made with Turkish tobacco by S Anargyros, a cigarette company of New York. The brand was introduced in 1892 but by 1913, Lorillard was making them.

OLD GOLD – an American brand owned by Lorillard.

PALL MALL – introduced in 1899 by Butler & Butler Co. Acquired by American Tobacco Co in 1907. It is now made in the US by RJ Reynolds and outside the US by BAT.

PETER STUYVESANT – named after the last Dutch Director-General of New Netherland (later New York) from 1647 to 1664; now owned by BAT.

PHILIP MORRIS – the leading American tobacco company. Philip Morris Companies Inc. changed its name to Altria Group Inc in 2003.

PLAYER'S – the most popular brand in Britain in the 1930s. It was founded by John Player in Nottingham in 1877 and merged as part of the Imperial Tobacco Group in 1901. There are many different Player brands: Gold Leaf, No6, John Player Special and Navy Cut.

RJ REYNOLDS – founded in 1874, now the second-largest tobacco company in the United States, manufacturing about one of every three cigarettes sold in the country.

ROTHMAN'S – founded in 1890 in London. Merged with BAT in 1999.

SILK CUT – the best selling brand in Britain in the 1990s as smokers switched to lower-tar brands; owned by Gallaher.

STATE EXPRESS 555 – originally produced by Adrath Tobacco Co Ltd and now owned by BAT. This is BAT's most popular brand in China.

THREE NUNS – originally produced by Stephen Mitchell & Son, Glasgow which was part of the Imperial Tobacco Company.

VIRGINIA SLIMS – introduced in 1968 by Philip Morris in America.

WILLS & CO – established in 1789 and became part of Imperial Tobacco in 1901. The Wills name brand was withdrawn in Britain in 1988 but is still sold in India.

WINSTON – an American brand which was introduced in 1954 by RJ Reynolds and became the best selling brand in the United States in the late 1960s.

WOODBINE – originally made by Wills but now made by Gallaher. An unfiltered cigarette extremely popular in the early 20th century.

BIBLIOGRAPHY

AMERICAN COLLEGE OF CHEST PHYSICIANS (2004) *Brief history of tobacco advertising to women* http://speakerskit.chestnet.org/wgtlc/history/p1.php

BARNARD, E F (1929) 'The cigarette has made its way up in society', *New York Times*, 9 June 1929

BLUM, Alan (1988) *Tobacco industry sponsorship of sports*, www.tobaccodocuments.org

BURNETT, Leo (1958) 'The Marlboro Story', *New Yorker Magazine*, 15 November 1958, Vol.34

DOLL, R and HILL, A B (1950) 'Smoking and carcinoma of the lung: preliminary report', *British Medical Journal*, ii, 1950

ERNSTER, Virginia (1985) 'Mixed messages for women, a social history of cigarette smoking and advertising', *New York State Journal of Medicine*, part 85, 1985

FISCHER, P M, SCHWARTZ, M P, RICHARDS, J W Jr, GOLDSTEIN, A O, And ROJAS, T H (1991) 'Brand recognition by children aged 3 to 6 years…', JAMA, December 11 1991

GILMAN, Sander L and ZHOU XUN (2004) *Smoke, a global history of smoking*, Raktion Books, London

GREAVES, Lorraine (1996) *Smoke Screen: Women's smoking and social control*, Fernwood Publishing, Canada

HEGARTY, John (1998) 'Selling the product' in *Power of the poster*, ed. Timners, Margaret, V&A Publications

HILTON, Matthew (2000) *Smoking in British popular culture*, Manchester University Press

KLUGER, Richard (1996) *Ashes to Ashes, America's hundred-year cigarette war, the public health, and the unabashed triumph of Philip Morris*, Knopf, New York